I0116667

The Synthesis Revolution:

New Thinking for a New Era of Prosperity

Thomas A. Rossman

EUDAIMONIA PUBLISHING

New York

Copyright © 2012 Thomas A. Rossman. All Rights Reserved.

"Tree of Synthesis" artwork on cover by Nick Lu. Copyright ©
2012 Thomas A. Rossman and Nick Lu. All Rights Reserved.

No part of this book may be sold, reproduced, utilized,
distributed or transmitted in any form or by any means without
written consent from the author, except for the inclusion of
brief quotations in a review.

Published by:

Eudaimonia Publishing LLC
29 Chase Road, #145
Scarsdale, NY 10583
www.EudaimoniaPublishing.com
info@EudaimoniaPublishing.com

ISBN: 0-9856596-0-2
ISBN-13: 978-0-9856596-0-8

NOTE: The author is available for interviews, speaking and
presenting this material to groups. For more information,
please contact us:

The Synthesis Revolution
www.SynthesisRevolution.com
Tom@SynthesisGroup.com

CONTENTS

Introduction: Foundations of Perpetual Improvement, Progress and Prosperity

Just over two centuries ago, recognizing the enormous potential of modern thinking about society and new methods of both exercising and restraining authority, the Framers of the U.S. Constitution set out to "form a more perfect Union." Their confidence in the potential to improve society was an expression of the belief, first articulated by John Locke, that individuals possessed not only the God-given right, but also the innate ability, to organize and govern themselves more effectively than a distant, divinely appointed monarch. Their approach was driven by the modern idea that well-balanced and inclusive political and economic institutions would empower a unified society to unleash the innovation and productivity of free individuals, thereby generating immense prosperity, while at the same time maintaining the cohesive stability of the broader community. This fundamental framework of Enlightenment principles, so skillfully synthesized in the enduring document that they produced, provided the foundation for America's enormous success and the inspiration for many nations around the world.

The Founding Fathers thoroughly understood that they were a unique part of the considerably larger trend of accelerating human progress and prosperity. Since the earliest hunter-gatherers first discovered how to cooperate, people have been striving to find new ways to better their lives, and then build upon that knowledge to help them rise above the pervasive scarcity and conflict that has defined much of human history. Even though there were limited periods of sustained development, it was not until the dawn of the modern age in Europe during the seventeenth and eighteenth centuries that progress and prosperity began a permanent upward trajectory. This unparalleled transformation was achieved by advancing beyond the narrow, one-dimensional ideas that had constrained European development for over a thousand years, and by adopting an entirely new way of thinking objectively about the world. As this new form of thinking took hold, a more effective method of analyzing the world based on actual observation, evidence, and experimentation led to groundbreaking discoveries and the implementation of durable solutions to previously intractable problems. The Founding Fathers successfully employed these new forms of thinking and analysis by taking what was useful and productive from both ancient and early modern thought, and combining it with a bold and decisive focus on how to improve the lives of every citizen of the newly united States of America.

The remarkable success of America since those early days is a shining example of how much can be achieved when individuals and institutions function effectively together to advance the development and well being of society. Yet as we continue to benefit from the enlightened discourse and framework established by the Founding Fathers, the dialogue and dynamic that drives our political system today has lost much of the productive energy and unified focus on solving difficult problems that guided and inspired the earlier debates. The way that we presently make critical decisions about the form and function of our governing institutions and the role of individuals has largely abandoned the fundamental method of perpetual improvement upon which modern progress and prosperity were built: objective observation and analysis, systematically examining the evidence to identify what is useful and effective in solving problems and promoting prosperity, and validation of potential solutions through experimentation and testing. Worse still, far from coming together to have a productive debate about meaningful ways to advance the country, the current trajectory of America portends even greater polarization on virtually every level of society: politically, economically, culturally, socially, and demographically. In fact, according to the Pew Research Center, political polarization, a key contributor to our present deficit of productive reconciliation, has nearly doubled over the past twenty-five years. In addition, with increasing social and economic disparities, the chasm between different groups in America is nearing unbridgeable proportions.

For over two decades, increasingly divided ideological and partisan coalitions have compromised our ability to have the productive dialogue that would lead to meaningful, lasting political and economic reforms. In many areas that are so vital to our continued growth and the expansion of prosperity, there is widespread agreement by Americans from all perspectives of the need for substantial reform and improvement to our competitive position in the world. For example, there are many issues that demand urgent attention: high school graduation rates and general educational performance, skyrocketing health care costs and the overall quality of care, rapid growth of unfunded entitlement obligations, inadequate immigration policies, the narrowing of economic opportunity for middle and lower income workers, tax policies, regulatory policies, and the deficits and debt that plague local, state, and federal governments. Furthermore, there is a serious need to understand and resolve the ongoing financial and economic policy confusion in the aftermath of the 2008 crisis.

We will not change and cannot alter the consistently poor results of our current political dynamic until we consciously and proactively transform the way that we make decisions on these crucial issues. For America to break free of this vicious cycle of polarization and refocus our efforts on making meaningful political and economic progress, we must overcome the narrow, one-dimensional thinking and dysfunctional interaction that so completely dominates our current political and economic debate.

The new thinking of the Synthesis Revolution is a return to the objective pursuit of, and intense focus on, solving difficult problems and removing the obstacles to even greater progress and prosperity. This is no small task given that society today is more complex and dynamic than ever. At the same time, we have vastly more sophisticated tools for understanding this complexity and the rapidly changing global conditions, but these tools are only beneficial if we consciously remove the substantial obstructions to their effective use. This new thinking is based on the understanding that both the energy of individual actions and the corresponding patterns of interdependence of these individuals are essential to an accurate grasp of any modern society. Both the emergent properties that result from the bottom-up forces of entrepreneurial drive and individual initiative, and the organizational connections viewed from the top-down such as the rule of law and pluralistic institutions that facilitate free, impartial market competition, are vital to a complete understanding of how society functions most productively.

Our ongoing pursuit of "forming a more perfect Union" is in need of serious reform; that reform begins with the new thinking of the Synthesis Revolution, which objectively and systematically takes what is good and useful from each of the various political perspectives and substantially broadens our view of the potential avenues to solving pressing problems of the world that are so plainly evident. It also provides the mechanism to achieve the vital function of electing leaders that are held accountable for the results of their policies and that continually adapt to new and changing circumstances. Any impediment that distorts our ability to accurately and objectively view the challenges and potential solutions or that disconnects our debate from the real world that we all inhabit and experience every day in favor of some theoretical, ideological, or idealized version of reality will continue to lower our productive potential, both as individuals and as a nation. The Synthesis Revolution will unite the vast group of concerned Americans who recognize the inability of the ideas and the leadership from both of the leading ideological and partisan coalitions to solve the very real and acute problems facing our nation today. One of the areas in which the Synthesis Revolution will have a tremendous impact is in resolving the critical dysfunction in the financial and economic policy arena that continues to lower our potential for growth and prosperity.

There are three primary barriers to the type of open, objective discourse and productive reconciliation envisioned by the Framers of our Constitution. These self-imposed obstructions are presently diverting our attention, diluting our focus, and preventing us from creating the most innovative, productive, and inclusive society possible. The first barrier is ideology, which actively distorts how decision makers on both sides view and perceive the world by shackling their political and economic thinking to an unwavering set of initial assumptions and predetermined conclusions. Over time, ideology has devolved from its original purpose as a useful mechanism for like-minded groups of individuals to pursue progress, into a tool for rigidly polarizing adherents of differing perspectives. The second barrier is partisan tribalism, or as

George Washington called it, the "Spirit of Party," whose potency depends on loyal supporters who map their identities to a particular group and which thrives on a zero-sum mentality of gaining and maintaining positions of power. The third barrier is the productivity-draining influence of special interests, which further polarizes and undermines the ability of both individual citizens and their leaders to sustain the prosperity, stability, and strength of our nation.

Taken together, the most negative impact of this self-reinforcing cycle of polarization is the progressive erosion of leadership and accountability at all levels of government. The further apart the two sides grow, the greater the paralysis, and the less necessary it is for either side to actually solve any problems and deliver on promises of growth and progress since those failures do not impede electoral success. Indeed, even with Congressional approval ratings close to single digits, the current level of accountability is so low that the vast majority of the members of both parties will get re-elected, regardless of the ineffectiveness of their actions and policies.

There is a growing frustration from all perspectives that this flawed dynamic is so entrenched that meaningful change is beyond our grasp. This is where the Synthesis Revolution steps into the breach and provides both the mechanism and the know-how to empower Americans to shift the energy and focus of our political and economic decision making back to solving problems and providing the foundation for even greater success.

Americans broadly understand the significant challenges confronting our nation today and want to see substantial reform. In many ways, the core issues are remarkably clear-cut: we want our political system and our leaders to promote a framework of organization in which our society can generate the greatest amount of prosperity and enable everyone to maximize their potential, both individually and as a nation. There is profound agreement and understanding among people of all perspectives and parties that we must reform our approach to confront this growing polarization if we are going to maintain our standard of living in an increasingly competitive world. The core challenge, however, is that our present political and economic dynamic lacks the necessary open, objective thinking and methodological tool kit to inspire and enact needed reforms. Presently, many Americans are searching for the framework of thinking and discourse that will lead us to meaningfully reverse this negative political and economic trajectory, and develop the unified approach and clarity of objectives that are so urgently required. For that, we need to think in new ways about the problems we face, not outsource our thinking to ideologies, political parties, or special interests, and begin to interact with each other more productively on the basis of how we can most effectively solve problems and improve the everyday lives of Americans on all levels. The hard fact is that there are no quick fixes or silver bullets that will somehow solve these formidable challenges overnight, but it will take the commitment of a broad group of Americans who are willing to look honestly and objectively at the challenges we face as a nation.

What is needed first is a mechanism for Americans to embrace the new thinking by shifting our political and economic focus to solving the pressing, real-world problems of the nation, overcoming the barriers that distort our debate, and restoring the conditions for further progress and prosperity. Secondly, we need a new method of political interaction to convert that focus into implementing these solutions, creating value, and productively unleashing the full dynamism of the American people. Only with such an approach will we enact the necessary reforms and produce the quality of leadership and accountability required to address our substantial and growing challenges. Given today's playing field, this is nothing short of revolutionary. At the same time, the transformational aspect of this approach lies in the ability to rise above all of the initial assumptions and predetermined conclusions of the currently polarized sides, and return to observing and analyzing the world objectively as it is. Only then can we realize our full potential and solve intractable problems, resolve longstanding impasses, and create new ways for perpetual improvement. As such, this process entails breaking down existing barriers, embracing new forms of thinking and interaction, and synthesizing both. This revolutionary proposition can be more accurately characterized as a "Synthesis Revolution."

America was the first nation to be founded on a set of ideas. Consequently, it has always been far more important for us than for any other country to remain true to the spirit of the Founding Fathers in "forming a more perfect Union" by thinking and interacting in effective ways. As Americans, we pride ourselves on embracing modern ideas and pursuing the most efficient, productive ways to solve problems. In other words, when something is clearly wrong, we fix it. This has been a distinguishing characteristic of America since the Founding Fathers and the early days of our Republic. However, in many major areas essential to our continued success, such as banking and finance, health care, tax policy, and education, we have allowed massive inefficiencies to creep in and substantially lower our productive potential. The new thinking and new method of the Synthesis Revolution are vital for the changes we need to make because this approach recognizes, as the Framers did, the importance of combining the top-down organizational framework of the rule of law and free and fair competition on the one hand, with the bottom-up forces of innovation, individual vitality, and entrepreneurial drive on the other. The successful productive reconciliation, or "synthesis," of these complementary forces has generated enormous prosperity throughout our country's history and can continue to do so for years to come. The result of this ongoing success is an unshakable confidence in our possession of the ability to improve our lives, both individually and as a nation. The Synthesis Revolution will solidify this foundation for the next step in our ascending prosperity.

PART I: How We Think Matters

To appreciate why such a revolutionary re-thinking is necessary today, we must first turn to how thinking and interaction in political development and debate shape our understanding of the world and how we choose to engage it.

The World We Have Created is a Product of Our Thinking

Despite the unprecedented accumulation of knowledge and advancement over the past 230 years, America once again finds itself at a crucial inflection point. Unlike most sectors of the American economy, our political dynamic has consistently failed to improve or productively evolve over the past several decades. Consequently, it has become much more of a drag on our prosperity than a positive contributor to it. Specifically, our current political dynamic is failing to effectively reconcile competing factions and diverging interests within the country or to produce the quality of leadership needed to deal with the substantial challenges of the twenty-first century. Most disturbingly, the current political dynamic is such that our leaders fail to even competently manage the institutions of government so thoughtfully devised by the Founding Fathers and subsequent generations of leaders. A good tree bears good fruit, yet even a cursory glance at the poor economic performance of the last decade, coupled with several longer-term negative trends such as stagnant median incomes, falling median net worth, and weak job creation, clearly illustrates the urgent need to structurally reform our approach and address the root causes of this negative trajectory.

President George Washington was not considered the most stirring orator or highly educated of the Founding Fathers; however, as a gifted leader, he possessed that rare quality which gave him a profound understanding of the power of government and of the type of leadership needed to effectively employ that power. In 1790 he said, "Government is not reason, it is not eloquence, it is force; like fire, a troublesome servant and a fearful master. Never for a moment should it be left to irresponsible action." The father of our country prophetically warning of "irresponsible action" by our elected officials is highly applicable to our current challenges.

President Washington would have undoubtedly opposed two specific forms of "irresponsible action" being perpetrated in the halls of power today. One is proactive, and occurs when various types of organizations, special interest groups, or companies hire armies of lobbyists and fund political campaigns in a bid to directly influence legislation, regulation, and the degree of oversight they are subject to. The other is reactive, and emerges when politicians make lavish, unfunded promises of future benefits and services, leaving the next generation to deal with the costs. With exploding unfunded entitlements, declining educational performance, skyrocketing medical costs, and a dysfunctional financial sector, Americans are wondering how our political dynamic has drifted so far away from addressing these critical problems to our currently unsustainable trajectory, and further, where the leadership is that remains so vital to our continued success. What remaining faith many Americans still had in the competing worldviews promoted by today's dominant political ideologies and parties has been violently unmoored by the ongoing financial crisis and polarized dysfunction in Washington. Yet our political leaders continue to engage in the same stale and meaningless squabbles, while allowing serious challenges to continually languish. Consequently, many Americans have understandably grown frustrated at the lack of effective leadership on either side. The distressing long-term uncertainty and growing anger people are experiencing today is born of the realization that the ideas and theories currently dominating the political and economic debate are incomplete at best, and thoroughly ineffective at worst. Instead of continuing the good work of our Founding Fathers in the ongoing process of "forming a more perfect Union," we are allowing political polarization and partisan division to lower our potential, both individually and as a nation.

Alexis de Tocqueville observed in the first volume of his widely respected nineteenth-century analysis of the United States that, "The greatness of America lies … in her ability to repair her faults." This fundamental character trait of solving problems is why, as daunting as our current political challenges may be, the future of America is amazingly bright. In fact, despite the glaring flaws in our political dynamic, America is positioned far better than any other nation to take advantage of new technology, innovation, and development around the world and continue our ascent and leadership through the twenty-first century and beyond.

The reason for such unbridled optimism is that unlike the vast majority of other nations today, America has the capability to proactively and consciously reform the way we think about these problems and the way we interact with one another to produce solutions, create value, and provide insightful leadership. As Albert Einstein incisively observed, "The world we have created is a product of our thinking; it cannot be changed without changing our thinking." Simply put, the greatest enemies to our future prosperity and continued leadership around the world are the distorting and unproductive elements of our current political dynamic, the influence of ideologies, political parties, and special interests, which confine our thinking to narrow, one-dimensional views and polarize our dialogue by diverting our focus away from solving problems and providing the foundation for prosperity and growth. These are significant barriers to a free, fair, and productive political and economic discourse, and require nothing short of engaging in new thinking and applying a new method of interaction. The Synthesis Revolution is the engine for propelling this fundamental change.

The Modern Miracle: New Ways of Thinking and Interacting Create New Forms of Prosperity

A closer inspection of the drivers of the profound political, economic, and societal transformation that rocked Europe in the preceding two centuries offers a powerful narrative for the importance of embracing new ways of thinking and interacting.

Prior to 1800, the vast majority of humanity struggled to rise even marginally above subsistence. Certain societies discovered comparative and competitive advantages that allowed them to grow and develop beyond their contemporaries, but as new challenges arose, these societies inevitably failed to successfully adapt, and fell into stagnation and decline. This cycle unfolded repeatedly over the course of thousands of years, until the emergence of the modern age in the seventeenth and eighteenth centuries.

As Europe climbed out of the medieval quagmire, it inspired and assisted whole sections of the globe in gradually rising above the threshold of scarcity for the first time. In fact, as we learned to apply modern ways of thinking and new methods of objective analysis and interaction, the world, as a whole, created more prosperity and more advances in science, medicine, longevity, and well-being than in all previous periods of history combined. This began gradually over the course of the early modern period by creating broad-based political and economic institutions and new forms of interaction needed for improving society and directing the overall focus to innovation, productivity, and inclusiveness.

To fully appreciate the significance of this unprecedented surge in human progress, consider that, according to the highly respected economist J. Bradford DeLong, the inflation-adjusted economic output per capita of the world in 5000 BCE was approximately $130. By the year 1800, 6,800 years later, output had not yet doubled, reaching a mere $250 per person. However, in the following 200 years alone, output accelerated to a staggering $8,175 per person. Again, putting that into context, despite a nearly seven-fold increase in population over the nineteenth and twentieth centuries, the output per person rose more than 3,200 percent in just two centuries, after rising just over 90 percent in the previous seven thousand years. All of this was accomplished by shifting the focus to observing the world and determining objectively what actually worked and what didn't work, and then building upon that knowledge to exponentially accelerate development.

When we realize how profound and unique this achievement was, the question then becomes: what has actually worked in the past and contributed to this extraordinary progress and prosperity and what has clearly not; and further, how might those experiences provide insight to help us address our urgent need to reform and improve our current political and economic dynamic?

The Origins of Polarization

There have always been very different perspectives on

how to approach the process of discovery and analysis. In many respects, polarization has consistently been present in one form or another throughout history, but the key to progress has been whether or not the dominant thinkers and political leadership of the day find a way to effectively analyze the contributions of competing perspectives and productively reconcile the differing views by taking what is useful from all sides and discarding what is not. The debate surrounding the construction and adoption of the U.S. Constitution still stands today as one of the greatest examples of the power of this solutions-based approach in the face of passionate differences in perspective.

Since the earliest days of Western thought in ancient Greece, the various perspectives of and approaches to discovery and analysis largely coalesced around two general points of view. One focused on a top-down worldview, and was represented by the analysis of great thinkers such as Pythagoras and then Plato: they looked at the world from an ideal and collective perspective and then observed the world through that lens. The other focused on a bottom-up approach, as evidenced in the thinking of leading scholars such as Heraclitus and then Aristotle: they first considered the evidence of the human senses and then extrapolated more idealized forms of organization and behavior out of their consideration of that view. Over time, both perspectives generated insightful observations, but have also proven vulnerable to that very human tendency of allowing one's initial claims and predetermined viewpoints to supersede the evidence at hand. Historically, the more these tendencies remained unaltered and unchallenged over long periods of time, the more entrenched the systems of thought became and the more they grew stagnant and unproductive as mechanisms for genuine discovery and improvement of the world. For example, Aristotelian scholasticism was a heroic effort by Thomas Aquinas and other late medieval scholars to introduce logical methods of deduction and reason to the theologically based worldview of their day. Whereas it was a valid attempt to expand knowledge, it also contained significant errors masquerading as universal truth. As a result, over time, it became a substantial barrier to genuine discovery of the world and was used to suppress open-ended political and scientific discourse and analysis.

In fact, following the collapse of ancient Greece and Rome, Western Civilization was stuck in a seemingly endless cycle of self-reinforcing mediocrity. During the medieval period it was the Chinese, Mongolian, and Islamic civilizations that flourished, spawning many great scientists, inventors, and philosophers; those empires were able to innovate and expand much more effectively than European society. Their continued expansion and growth in Asia and the greater Middle East was impressive, while the majority of Europe remained largely insular, bouncing along the threshold of scarcity, just one or two bad harvests away from widespread deprivation.

Throughout this period, societies that were unified, yet remained open to new ideas, prospered and expanded. But when those very same societies began to erect barriers and close themselves off, they stagnated and eventually began to decline. For example, during the Song dynasty of the tenth through twelfth centuries, China experienced rapid economic, technological, and trade expansion, making it the wealthiest and most developed civilization on earth. However, just a few centuries later in the Ming dynasty, just as European explorers and scholars were beginning to push their traditional boundaries, an inward shift and restrictions on trade and exchange initiated a long period of decline. In a greater sense, this is the story of all human civilization. When societies are open, allowing themselves to continually adjust and successfully adapt to changing circumstances, they thrive; when they are not, stagnation and decay are never far behind.

The key difference between humanity's recent success and that of the preceding eras was the development of a new way of objectively thinking about the world and the adoption of new methods for investigating how the world and society actually work, breaking free of the closed loop of narrow, one-dimensional thinking and the accumulated assumptions and superstitions of previous eras. Toward the end of the medieval period, Europe began to return to, and in fact improve upon, the classical spirit of open-ended inquiry, discovery, and objective re-examination of how societies thought about the world and interacted with one another.

The Birth of the Modern Era: Discovering the Real World

After an incubation period in the Renaissance, the medieval worldview was gradually replaced by new ideas on all fronts: scientific, theological, sociological, philosophical, and eventually, even political and economic. This renewal of the desire to objectively discover the way in which the world actually works and to look at new and improved ways of engaging in human affairs, as opposed to the reliance on increasingly disproven theoretical assumptions, yielded tremendous results. Instead of living in fear of the arbitrary whims of nature or of a tyrannical ruler, people began to harness aspects of the natural world and of human affairs to enable both individuals and society as a whole to flourish and live far better than had ever previously been imagined. Indeed, this was the age of discovery, the Scientific Revolution, the age of reason, the Commercial and Industrial Revolutions and, with the Enlightenment, the birth of modern democratic societies. The world has continued to enjoy the benefits of these advances and to improve upon them ever since.

It was during the Renaissance and age of discovery that European thinkers became more open to new ideas re-emerging from the ancient past as well as from far-flung parts of the contemporary world. These new concepts challenged earlier assumptions and preconceived notions of how things actually worked, inspiring in the process an enormous amount of energy, appetite, and curiosity for further inquiry. Gradually, the realization took hold that the insular thinking and narrow ideas of the Middle Ages were more of a barrier than a catalyst to uncovering actual, objective truth.

As Copernicus, Galileo, and others exposed the flaws in medieval scholarship, it became apparent that discovering new ways of effectively thinking about the world and applying those ideas for the betterment of society required a new method of objective, open-ended investigation. Indeed, a new approach for channeling this enormous energy unleashed by the new ways of thinking first emerged in the field of science with the development of the scientific method by great men such as Francis Bacon, Galileo, Descartes, and Newton. This new method of objective investigation directly resulted in the tectonic surge of discovery during the Scientific Revolution of the seventeenth and eighteenth centuries. Then, the new thinking of Thomas Hobbes, John Locke, and other Enlightenment figures initiated a similar degree of groundbreaking progress in the political and economic spheres. They advocated a new method of inclusive democratic interaction and engagement, which eventually resulted in the political and economic revolutions of the same time period.

From the end of the sixteenth century on, Western thinkers increasingly began to understand how important consistent methodology was in the processes of thinking, discovering, and interacting. Both Bacon and Hobbes contributed greatly to this new understanding by pointing out that "knowledge itself is power," and that it could be built upon to provide meaningful improvement in the way humanity experienced the world in the scientific as well as the political realms. Bacon further asserted that an effective, disciplined method was superior to genius because a brilliant person on the wrong path only succeeds in getting farther away from genuine discovery more rapidly.

Out of this emerging cumulative body of knowledge and experience, Western countries gradually embraced free, fair, and productive political discourse and established the corresponding institutions of government that facilitated the exchange of ideas and effectively channeled power, which provided the framework for accelerating progress and prosperity. The accumulated insights of two centuries of new thinking applied through new methods resulted in the foundational documents of all modern political thought: the British Bill of Rights, the United States Declaration of Independence and Constitution, and the French Declaration of the Rights of Man and of the Citizen. Furthermore, the Declaration of Independence and United States Constitution were unique contributors to this process by both blazing trails and becoming models and sources of inspiration to the world that every society, young and old, could embrace and use to meaningfully improve the world in which they lived.

PART II: Barriers to Productive Thinking and Reconciliation

The Human Tendency to Idealize Systems of Thought

As the founders of these great advances understood, the origin of modern progress was embracing the new thinking of objectivity to differentiate between what was real and what was merely speculation or superstition. The conscious and proactive focus on objective analysis opened up vast new areas of discovery, which fed a growing belief in humankind's ability to understand and improve the world around them. This drive for improvement then resulted in the adoption of new methodologies and institutions to lay a broad foundation for even greater advancement in the future.

While new methods of thinking and investigation born of the modern era led to an explosion of discovery, it also became clear, once again, that systems of thought were subject to that other natural human inclination to idealize a preferred way of thinking about, investigating, and validating what we observe and perceive. As scholars had done since the beginning of Western thought, many important thinkers resisted an open-ended approach focused on objective observation and critical thinking, and clung to a narrow, one-dimensional perspective of rigidly inflexible thinking. This has been the case throughout history and remains true today. Like a healthy cell in the body of ideas that mutates into a cancerous one, this negative human tendency expands and grows alongside the positive aspects of discovery, becoming chronically entrenched in the outlook and often overtaking the healthier approach to inquiry. This cancerous disease can be described as our consistent propensity to replace the continual search for new discoveries and new ways of improving existing ideas with the misplaced confidence that ultimate and final truth has been revealed. Stephen Hawking, one of the world's leading physicists, summarizes the problem this way: "The greatest enemy of knowledge is not ignorance; it is the illusion of knowledge." In our current political dynamic, ideological and partisan coalitions are both driven by a powerful "illusion of knowledge" that represents a formidable challenge to discovering real knowledge focused on solving difficult problems and generating more prosperity.

Idealized systems of thought, such as the various types of ideology, introduce self-imposed barriers to true knowledge and understanding by replacing creative thought and objective, open investigation with a collection of initial assumptions and pre-determined conclusions. Over time, these presuppositions gradually and often imperceptibly morph into rationalizations and justifications based not on observation and evidence of the real world, but on how firmly they reinforce the ends and entrenched beliefs of the idealized systems themselves. As previously mentioned, Aristotelian Scholasticism extolled the divine virtues of human logic and reason, but nevertheless asserted that the earth was the center of the universe. This assumption inspired centuries of scholastic astronomers to develop increasingly more elaborate ways to explain the "illusion of knowledge" that the sun, the planets, and all of the other stars revolved around the earth. The beguiling appeal, that alluring false symmetry between what a system of thought claims to know by initial assumption and pre-determined conclusion, and what is actually known based on objective observation and evidence, is what continues to make them so dangerous and distorting to our understanding of and ability to improve the daily lives of individuals and society.

THOMAS A. ROSSMAN

The Birth of Ideology: Idealized Systems of Thought on Steroids

As modern society began to change ever more rapidly at the end of the eighteenth century and political inclusiveness began to expand, various systems of thought emerged to assist a wider audience in making sense of these rapid shifts. This new breed of idealized systems of thought was so potent and expanded so quickly that an entirely new word was required to define them. It was a late eighteenth-century French aristocrat, Antoine-Louis-Claude, Comte Destutt de Tracy, who first coined the term *ideology*, with the intent of conceiving a new "science of ideas." The original purpose of this new science of ideas was to apply the innovative developments in political thought to actually improve society, similar to the way that Bacon urged the application of the extraordinary advances of the Scientific Revolution to improve daily life on every level of society. As they evolved, however, various ideologies began to exhibit their increasingly idealized positions as the embodiment of progress itself, instead of, as they were originally intended, a mechanism for pursuing progress.

As they matured over the course of the nineteenth century, these new ideologies dismantled the necessary guardrails that had guided and directed open-ended inquiry and productive thinking. Ideology quickly became a vehicle for herding people with different perspectives into differing camps and defending established positions. Opposing ideologies erected substantial barriers to productive debate, even going so far as to develop very different definitions of fundamental principles such as liberty, justice, and fairness. Competing ideologies actively promoted partisan clashes by merging sentiments, pre-analytic notions and different, naturally occurring perspectives into opposing, one-size-fits-all worldviews because such battles were perfectly suited to mobilizing large portions of the expanding voter franchise. People no longer needed to worry about the burden of thinking for themselves; instead, they just needed to map their respective identities to an ideology and act accordingly. Adherence to an ideology thus channeled the energy of its supporters away from debating solutions to the real, pressing problems of the times, and toward the vulgar and unproductive pursuit of winning political battles and gaining partisan power.

In the best case, this had the cumulative effect of draining a good deal of efficiency and productivity from the political dialogue in Western societies. In the worst case, the most virulent ideologies, such as Nationalism, Fascism, and Communism, have led to incredibly destructive wars and the pinnacle of inhumanity in the form of genocide, mass imprisonment, and the wholesale starvation of their own adherents. In fact, according to Dr. R.J. Rummel, the widely-respected political scientist and expert on mass violence, in the twentieth century, ideologically driven murders by governments outnumbered the casualties of military warfare by more than two to one. Yet even in their milder form, ideologies spawn significant barriers to the pursuit of progress, prosperity, and well-being. Ideology and the related factors of partisan tribalism and special interests have become the three primary impediments to vital productive reconciliation and the transformation of our current political dynamic.

Barrier I - Clashing Ideologies in the Political Dynamic

As society has become increasingly complex over the past two centuries, ideology has developed into a formidable barrier, preventing us from realizing the promise of modernity and of the Founding Fathers to develop the most innovative, productive, and inclusive society possible. Indeed, competing ideologies reductively transform legitimately different perspectives into ridiculous caricatures of themselves, rendering real debate functionally impossible.

Both worldviews, top-down and bottom-up, offer important insights into how the real world operates, and both are essential to understanding the complexity of modern political and economic conditions. The top-down view, common to ideologies of the Left, has focused on the view of society as a whole, humanity's potential for perfectibility, and how problems can be addressed through collective or government action. This thinking originated toward the end of the Enlightenment with the writings of Jean-Jacques Rousseau, and became the animating force of the great continental thinkers of the French Revolution and German philosophy. The bottom-up perspective, common on the Right side of today's political spectrum, has focused much more on the individual as the key unit of political activity and the engine of stability, gradual reform, and less centralized authority. More in line with the Anglo-American theorists, it drew inspiration from John Locke and Edmund Burke, and provided the rationale for the Glorious Revolution in England and the American revolutionaries. As these two general perspectives evolved into political movements from the late eighteenth century on, their differing visions of how society could most productively be structured and how it could most efficiently solve problems grew further and further apart.

Indeed, all of the ideological assumptions of both the Left and the Right are built on the simple and elegant myth that each particular group of like-minded partisans has discovered a comprehensive approach that solves all of society's problems. Our current political dynamic only perpetuates and reinforces this false claim, channeling money and power to each side. Even considering that within each camp there is wide divergence about what actually constitutes genuine ideological orthodoxy, adherents fiercely defend their claim to their rightful authority over how best to address issues, and conveniently ignore the unmistakable evidence that neither side is in possession of a monopoly on truth.

In the United States today, how could it ever be possible for two sides with very different definitions of core terms such as *freedom* and *liberty*, reinforced by ideological rigidity, to have a productive dialogue? As is demonstrated every day by what passes for genuine debate on virtually every level of our political dynamic, such a dialogue is not possible. The two increasingly polarized ideologies have corralled many Americans into narrow, one-dimensional views of society. Each ideology has become a self-imposed barrier to the ability to see the world as it really is. The sad result is that we are left with a considerably narrower set of potential solutions: the ones deemed acceptable by one side or the other, and the even smaller set deemed palatable by both.

As this voluntary limitation of ideas restricts our thinking about the real world, we have, in effect, replaced the pursuit of effective leadership with a willingness to settle for those who assert these false claims most eloquently, and those who demonize and demagogue their opposition most savagely. Both sides take solace in the repeated assertions that it is only the other side that engages in contradictions and hypocrisy, ignoring the substantial evidence of their own incoherence and failures. Political factions have eagerly embraced ideology as a means to gain and maintain power, which has only served to further disconnect our debate from reality and take our society even further away from a new era of productive prosperity.

Barrier II - The Spirit of Party: The Institutionalization of Political Ideologies, the Tribalization of Factions, and the Threat of Government by Plutocracy

In addition to ideological divisions, another barrier and source of polarization in our political dynamic is the tribalization of factions based on partisan division. Even though they have grown far worse in recent decades, these divisive forces have been at work in varying degrees since the beginning of our nation. President Washington, in his famous 1796 Farewell Address, insightfully and presciently warned of the destructive nature of a "Spirit of Party." He understood how deeply ingrained factionalism was in human behavior, describing it as "inseparable from our nature, having its root in the strongest passions of the human mind." At the same time, he also understood how destructive and deeply distorting factionalism could be to our political dynamic, observing that the two sides, driven by the Spirit of Party, "are likely, in the course of time and things, to become potent engines, by which cunning, ambitious and unprincipled men will be enabled to subvert the Power of the People, & to usurp for themselves the reins of Government, destroying afterwards the very engines which have lifted them to unjust dominion." Combined with the vigilance that Washington advocated earlier against "irresponsible action" by elected officials, it seems our first president deeply understood the challenges of leadership in a democratic society. In contrast, America today has two political parties that are clearly more intent on gaining power by usurping for themselves the reins of government than solving our difficult challenges.

Our future prosperity is currently under direct assault from this very same "Spirit of Party" that President Washington described so accurately. Today, our political system is a zero-sum game: one party's win is the other's loss. In this context, ideas viewed or labeled as post-partisan may sound appealing, but they are effectively meaningless. In the realization of President Washington's insightful prediction, in the all-consuming pursuit of the reins of government and political power, our current political parties are far too willing to ignore and delay serious discussion about significant challenges, while blaming the other side for shirking their responsibility to the nation.

President Theodore Roosevelt experienced a similar dynamic of partisan division in his day, but refused to pursue power through placation and demagoguery, as had been customary of early twentieth-century political figures. He stated unequivocally, "We stand equally against government by a plutocracy and government by a mob." President Roosevelt clearly demonstrated by his own actions that he would rather have an honest debate about the real problems confronting the country than outsource his integrity and leadership ability to the Spirit of Party. His stance was principled, brave, and not without consequence: his style of leadership alienated powerful political bosses and interest groups on both sides, costing him the election of 1912. Yet a growing number of Americans see through the veils of division, beyond ideology and partisanship, and long for that type of statesmanship and leadership today.

Barrier III - Special Interests: Self-Interest, Wrongly Understood

The reconciliation of substantial differences in interests and ideas between different groups within society has always been, and will always be, a necessary function in our political process. In an effective political dynamic, politicians and policymakers would objectively evaluate these interests and assess how well each one promoted innovation, productivity, and overall prosperity, just as the Framers had envisaged so insightfully. However, our hyper-polarized, ideologically driven political dynamic today has allowed special interest groups and rent-seeking coalitions, also commonly called distributional coalitions, to exercise disproportionate influence over the decision-making process in favor of narrowly defined issues and interests. These groups extract financial benefit not from building a productive enterprise or creating value through a new or improved product or service, but by manipulating rules, regulations, and lawmakers to favor one narrow group over the interests of the country. Their increasing power and influence enables them to feed off the accumulated prosperity Americans have amassed over the past two centuries, and reinforces the dysfunctional monopolies of our political and economic debates to the detriment of our well-being as individuals, and our competitive advantage as a nation.

Since the eighteenth century, when productivity and prosperity began to increase steadily, there have been those who have interpreted the emergence of individualism and self-interest as the engine for creating more prosperity and unleashing the dynamic potential of a free people, while others have viewed the emergence of individualism and self-interest as the rationale for pursuing the advancement of one person or a narrow group, regardless of the cost to the vast majority or the destruction of value to the wider society. In this one respect, the political and economic dynamic of society has changed very little in the past 250 years. The one notable exception is our ability today to more fully understand and recognize what generates value, and what merely distributes the value created by others.

This fundamental division in our current political and

economic dynamic is a serious flaw, and a byproduct of the widespread confusion and deliberate abuse of the concept of individualism and self-interest. The lack of a clear understanding of this important concept is the reason why narrow special interests and rent-seeking coalitions have gained so much influence over political debates and economic policies, and through their disproportionate power are making our society far less productive and considerably more vulnerable to unforeseen shocks than it should be.

In fact, as the modern notion of individualism became more firmly rooted in society over the course of the eighteenth and early nineteenth centuries, great thinkers such as the Founding Fathers, Adam Smith, and Alexis de Tocqueville recognized not only the enormous energy created by a free people pursuing individual success, but also the potential danger of individuals or narrow groups of people pursuing self-interest with reckless, unchecked abandon. In the Federalist Papers, most specifically Nos. 9 and 10, James Madison and Alexander Hamilton clearly recognized how unrestrained factional interests undermined the prosperity and stability of the classical democratic system of Greece and the republican system of Rome. At the same time, they firmly believed that the new method of a free, fair, and productive debate, along with checks and balances on power, could effectively channel that potentially destructive energy to positive ends.

Adam Smith also discussed how increasing the productivity of individual economic actions could benefit both the workers themselves and society as a whole. At the same time, Smith wrote extensively, passionately, and in great detail about how certain individuals and narrow groups have always sought to use their power and influence to tilt the balance of economic activity in their favor, to the detriment of society as a whole. It was these monopolistic tendencies on the part of both governments and narrow groups of politicians and businessmen that threatened to undermine the enormous economic gains Great Britain experienced in Smith's day. A century and a half later, F. A. Hayek would echo these same sentiments in observing that "the argument for liberty is not an argument against organization, which is one of the most powerful tools human reason can employ, but an argument against all exclusive, privileged, monopolistic organization, against the use of coercion to prevent others from doing better."

Several decades following Smith and the Founders, Alexis de Tocqueville wrote about these same trends in his famous book, *Democracy in America,* dedicating an entire chapter to the topic. The chapter was titled, tellingly, "How the Americans Combat Individualism by the Principle of Self-Interest Rightly Understood." He defined "self-interest rightly understood" as "some point on which private interest and public interest meet and amalgamate," and further described it as a process of reconciliation between diverging interests "by what means the inhabitants of the United States almost always manage to combine their own advantage with that of their fellow citizens." Like Hamilton, Madison, and Smith before him, de Tocqueville observed that factional discord and competing interests could be harnessed to promote the good of both individuals and society as a whole, arguing that self-interest rightly understood "checks one personal interest by another, and uses, to direct the passions, the very same instrument that excites them."

Today, we urgently need to re-embrace that spirit that de Tocqueville describes by directing our passions into providing the foundation by which individual actions can be rewarded and society as a whole can be consistently more prosperous and durable, instead of favoring special interests, factions, ideologies, or political parties. A good tree bears good fruit, and as so many insightful thinkers have consistently pointed out, allowing certain groups with political or financial power to distort our political and economic discourse and profit from it, no matter how little value they create or how much destruction they cause, is certainly not in the long-term interests of any nation.

The Framers envisioned channeling our energy and focusing our political and economic dynamic on what works, creates value, and generates prosperity, and away from what doesn't work and what merely carves up the value generated by others. By understanding this distinction and factoring it into our current political discourse through the Synthesis Revolution, we can significantly alter the way we address our challenges and take a major step toward turning around the negative political and economic trends weighing down our transition into a new era of prosperity.

PART III: Recent Evolution of America's Political and Economic Dynamic - The Rise of Unreconciled Factions and Interests and the Explosion of Polarization

In order to enact change and embrace serious reform, we must first appreciate where we stand today. The barriers to a free, fair, and productive debate have increased the polarization and deepened the divisions in our society, both politically and economically, ushering us closer to a new inflection point in our country's trajectory. Throughout our history, we have had a series of challenging inflection points. We have met each one of these challenges decisively, and in resolving the competing forces involved through productive reconciliation, we laid the groundwork for new eras of prosperity and inclusiveness. The Declaration of Independence led to the Revolution; the Constitution led to the enduring foundations of a new nation; the expansion of the voting franchise led to a more inclusive society; the Civil War led to the preservation of the Union and the abolition of slavery; the Second Industrial Revolution led to the establishment of a modern economy; the Progressive Era led to a more productive and inclusive economic system; and women's suffrage and the Civil Rights Movement provided the enfranchisement of vital segments of our society.

The Emergence of an Ideological Chasm in Late Twentieth-Century U.S. Politics

As our nation matured and expanded, the political dynamic continued to evolve; yet the story of its evolution throughout the twentieth century is about the developments that are leading us to a new inflection point. From the election of 1932 up to 1980, the Democratic Party held complete control of Congress for forty-four of those forty-eight years (and would continue to hold the House, uninterrupted, until the election of 1994). This was a period dominated by the so-called Roosevelt New Deal coalition, which advocated for an expansionist role of the state in the country's affairs. Interestingly, this thesis of active state intervention, which took government spending as a percentage of total output from just under 10 percent in the late 1920s to well over 20 percent today, was not exclusive to the Left: the three Republican Presidents of that period all participated in expanding the scope of the federal government. In fact, President Nixon, considered to be the most conservative of the three, famously declared himself to be a convert to Keynesianism and implemented wage and price controls, which was an extraordinary use of government power that would no doubt have earned him the label of "socialist" if he were to propose those measures today. The consensus for this top-down, active government thesis went unchallenged for nearly fifty years, until the stagflation of the 1970s and the Carter "malaise" created the space for an alternative perspective to gain preeminence.

Beginning in the early 1950s, a new ideological movement began to emerge with thinkers such as Russell Kirk and William F. Buckley, Jr. For the first time, a cogent intellectual and political movement on the Right was gradually coming together to confront the Roosevelt New Deal coalition. In 1980, President Reagan gave this growing movement its first taste of meaningful political power. He advocated a bottom-up, grassroots antithesis to the New Deal coalition thesis, seeing government as "the problem, not the solution." His powerful advocacy of this argument is why Reagan is still considered such a transformational leader today. What is lost in the rush to claim the political capital of his legacy is how meaningful the impact of his argument was to the core of our political dynamic. For the first time in nearly fifty years, there was a serious contest of clashing worldviews in the halls of power, and it is this conflict of perspective that we are still unsuccessfully attempting to reconcile today.

The Reagan bottom-up antithesis was not an opposition to government categorically; rather, it was a complex argument against the ever-expanding government thesis of the previous half-century. President Reagan believed the government was excessively consuming resources more efficiently left in the private sphere. He put it this way: "It is not my intention to do away with government. It is rather to make it work, work with us, not over us; stand by our side, not ride on our back. Government can and must provide opportunity, not smother it; foster productivity, not stifle it." In the great tradition of the Framers, President Reagan was attempting to "form a more perfect Union," from a perspective that not only aggressively confronted the unproductive aspects, but also incorporated the useful elements of the status quo of the previous fifty years.

Even though he was unmistakably committed to his conservative values, at the same time, President Reagan understood the profound difference between his own rhetoric and the realities of differing perspectives and a divided government. Since President Reagan left office and took with him the ability to personally reconcile these different perspectives and interests, the chasm between these two sides has grown to alarmingly dysfunctional proportions. For over two decades, we have been living in a society with an increasingly unresolved ideological war that has been reinforced and exacerbated by partisan tribalism and the influence of special interests. Today, instead of fostering innovation, productivity, and inclusiveness, our political dynamic is stuck between two idealized visions of the world: one top-down on the Left, and the other bottom-up on the Right. Both visions have demonstrated time after time that they are perfectly comfortable with allowing the conflict to persist unabated, thereby delaying difficult decisions and postponing serious political and economic reform.

More alarmingly, these forces of division are only gaining in strength as America continues to become more polarized, politically, economically, culturally, and socially. For example, in 1976, 27 percent of Americans lived in landslide counties in which one party defeated the other by more than 20 percent in the presidential election. By the election of 2008, the percentage of voters living in landslide counties increased to 48 percent, and the election of 2012 promises an even greater landslide division. Moreover, the polarization goes far beyond just the political sphere, and there are "landslide" characteristics in other categories as well. For example, in 2008, 89 percent of the Whole Foods stores in the United States were in counties carried by Barack Obama, while 62 percent of Cracker Barrel restaurants were in counties carried by John McCain. Furthermore, there is a growing body of evidence in cognitive and social science research and peer-reviewed scholarship that Left-leaning individuals and Right-leaning individuals have very different psychological and even physiological responses to the same set of political stimuli. In other words, their brains work in fundamentally different ways when perceiving and reacting to social and political situations. Given this core divide in how problems and solutions are understood, it is inconceivable that any one ideology or partisan platform could ever bridge this growing trend of polarization.

In fact, far from coming together and unifying in purpose, many leading sociologists from both sides believe that we are politically, economically, socially, and culturally, in the words of Charles Murray, "coming apart." These powerful forces of division and polarization are only driving people farther away from one another and making a productive reconciliation even more complex and difficult, if not impossible, to realize.

How Economic Policymaking and Regulatory Trends Have Reflected the Worst Aspects of our Failing Political Dynamic

The crossroads in our political sphere has meaningfully reduced productive reconciliation in our financial and economic policies as well. Many areas of the U.S. economy have undergone a similar lack of structural and regulatory reform, with opposing political forces exerting significant influence over how the country has regulated and managed its economic affairs. In particular, the story of the U.S. financial sector throughout the twentieth century is a case in point.

Following the 1929 stock market crash, and up until the early 1980s, Congress put in place a series of regulatory reforms to prevent another serious financial bubble from causing a repeat of the Great Depression. Those reforms were remarkably successful until the stagflation and skyrocketing interest rates of the late 1970s led to the across-the-board deregulation of savings and loan institutions (S&Ls). At that time, S&Ls were a cornerstone of local community finance, and they accounted for more than half of all home mortgages. After forty-five years of stability, in a little more than a decade following deregulation, more than 700 S&Ls went bankrupt, nearly 25 percent of the total. The fallout from the resulting scandal and crisis required a bailout that directly cost U.S. taxpayers between 100 and 200 billion dollars, and significantly contributed to the recession of the early 1990s.

Instead of learning valuable lessons from this policy failure through a productive dialogue, the reaction of legislators and policymakers was to reshuffle the existing regulatory bodies and continue with the same mentality of "cut, slash, chop" in every facet of our financial regulatory and oversight system. By the end of the 1990s, the Glass-Steagall Act, one of the pillars of the post-1929 reforms, and other important financial regulatory measures were repealed. These reckless decisions, along with other deregulatory efforts by the Federal Reserve, resulted in the creation of what are now known as the "too big to fail" banks. Furthermore, during the 1990s the over-leveraged and unregulated use of derivative securities led to a series of spectacular financial collapses, including the bankruptcy of Orange County, one of the richest counties in America, and the implosion of Long-Term Capital Management, one of the most prestigious hedge funds in the world. Despite these high-profile financial train wrecks, politicians from both political parties decided not to regulate the market for those same derivative securities, on the basis of the same flawed justifications. Thereafter, the opaque and poorly understood market for these "financial weapons of mass destruction," as Warren Buffett called them, grew rapidly from 50 trillion to over 600 trillion dollars in less than a decade.

More than 200 years ago, Adam Smith warned that "profit is always highest in the countries which are going fastest to ruin." He believed this because in a healthy economic framework, free and fair competition, in addition to transparency, would allow new entrants to keep costs low for consumers while continuing to improve quality, thereby benefiting everyone in society and contributing to what Smith called the conditions of "universal opulence." In 2006, the financial sector accounted for over 40 percent of the profits of the S&P 500, even though it accounted for less than 9 percent of overall economic output. In an economic system where financial companies provided effective intermediation and ensured productive allocation of capital, this unbalanced division of profit between the financial sector and the real economy would never happen. But in our polarized political and economic debate dominated by extremist ideologies, such imbalances, and the unnecessary vulnerability to the whole financial and economic system they produce, have not only become far too common, but are increasing in size and frequency.

Ultimately, the U.S. economy paid a steep price for the lax oversight of our financial system when the bubble burst in 2008. That self-imposed crisis has cost U.S. citizens over 7 trillion dollars in lost net worth and has caused a deep recession, the full extent of which is still not known. By comparison, the bursting of the internet, telecom, and technology bubble in 2000 resulted in losses of a few trillion dollars and the milder recession of 2001-2002. "Too big to fail" banks and the irresponsible use of unregulated derivatives were key components of the financial collapse. Nevertheless, barely four years after the crisis, the five largest banks in the United States are nearly 30 percent larger than they were prior to the crisis, and far more than twice the size they were when the Glass-Steagall Act and other regulations were gutted in 1999. In fact, each of the last three serious recessions directly followed the collapse of a financially driven bubble that involved serious fraud on the part of companies in the financial sector. Even after tepid attempts at reform, the now 700 trillion dollar derivatives market is still largely unregulated, and the consolidated banking institutions that had been at the heart of the crisis continue to get bigger.

Sadly, politicians on both sides are failing to engage in a meaningful debate about devising a durable regulatory framework, restoring stability to the system, or ensuring that it provides capital for innovation and industry efficiently, even though there is a growing chorus for reform among academics and many current and former regulators. Until we challenge our thinking and confront the dangerous ideology underpinning our current financial and regulatory policies and the still-evident structural inefficiencies, we will continue to flirt with financial chaos. In the meantime, our financial system will continue to allocate financial resources that are vital to our economy in very inefficient and unproductive ways.

That Which is Stronger Than All the Armies in the World

Today, as we confront the stagnation of our current political dynamic and the lack of effective leadership, we find that in many ways America is in a position not unlike Europe in the late Middle Ages. Granted, we are at a much higher level of prosperity and development than our ancestors and science has continued to advance, but our current political dynamic has devolved from providing a foundation for continued ascent to consistently draining our productive energy and resources. To a certain degree, we have reached what historians call a "hard ceiling" in our political development; this occurs when the dynamic energy of our institutions shifts from creating more prosperity to carving up the value generated by our forbears. Far too much of the creative problem solving energy of our society is presently being diverted to useless and counterproductive ends. Our current political dynamic has not only proven to be completely ineffective in solving problems for our society, but even worse, neither side is even marginally effective in basic management and oversight functions that should be elementary. Just like the powerful institutions of medieval times, the apparatus of our current political and economic power structure still clings to the failed ideas and the distorted views that maintain the status quo.

The weight of the evidence is overwhelming from the standpoint of many of the social science disciplines: sociology, cognitive science, economics, psychology, political science, and history. If there is one thing that is absolutely clear about our current situation from every angle, it is that ideology, partisan tribalism, and special interests provide an exceedingly weak foundation upon which to build a healthy and productive political and economic discourse. What, then, can fundamentally transform our political and economic dynamic?

Sir Isaac Newton believed, "There is one thing stronger than all the armies in the world; and that is an idea whose time has come." Just as the scientific and political revolutions of the early modern period were a byproduct of new ways of thinking and a new methodological approach for engaging in human affairs, thus laying the foundations of modern prosperity, so too will the new thinking and new methods of the Synthesis Revolution give rise to a New Era of Prosperity today. This revolution will dislodge the entrenched political and economic dynamic presently holding America hostage to failed ways of thinking and divisive forms of interaction. More specifically, the Synthesis Revolution is the mechanism by which we can restore a truly free, fair, and productive debate focused on solving urgent and pressing problems, creating value for future generations, and generating insightful leadership focused on innovation, productivity, and inclusiveness through a return to objective observation and analysis, systematically identifying what is good and useful, and validation through experimentation and testing.

PART IV: Time for a Revolution in How We Think and Interact

Modern society has resulted in the generation of tremendous prosperity and advancement for humankind, but it has also resulted in far more rapid change than during any preceding era. In scientific and sociological terms, it is a perfect example of a complex, adaptive system. As such, both the bottom-up forces that are in constant motion and the top-down patterns that vie for influence are equally vital to a genuine understanding of the whole system. In order to truly continue the work of the Founding Fathers in "forming a more perfect Union," we must be able to view, analyze, and gain an understanding of how individuals and society interact and operate from both perspectives.

The speed with which modern society and economies continue to change means that the risks and potential damage from ideological, partisan, and special interest forces is far greater than ever before, as evidenced in the 2008 financial crisis. Indeed, the fierce debate between the laissez-faire and the Keynesian visions of economic policy did not prevent the near collapse of our entire financial system, nor have these competing utopian visions prevented more than a decade of stagnation in median incomes, median net worth, and employment. Until we get beyond these structural barriers of accumulated assumptions and the failed conclusions of these systems of thought, our political dynamic will continue to be a drag on America's ability to innovate, prosper, and thrive.

The Synthesis Revolution is an empowering movement that brings together the enormous energy needed to shift our current political and economic focus back to the real world, as well as a methodology for channeling that energy into solving our substantial and growing challenges. Just as the scientific and political revolutions of the early modern period fostered new ways of thinking and a new approach for dealing with society's challenges, so too does the Synthesis Revolution create the understanding and the mechanism for improving our society today.

Bringing Fresh Thinking to the Chaos: Practicing Radical Objectivity

The first step is to embrace new thinking by tossing out all of the accumulated baggage of initial assumptions and predetermined conclusions from the failed systems of thought of the past era and adopt objective observation and analysis. Today, America's political and economic dynamic is being held captive to the failed ideas of the past. However, just as the early moderns discovered, discarding our working assumptions and familiar analyses creates another challenge: how do we make genuine discoveries of the way the world really works?

Francis Bacon, one of the early pioneers of the scientific method, believed that the core challenge of his day was nothing less than to "commence a total reconstruction of sciences, arts, and all human knowledge, raised upon the proper foundations." And even though different perspectives abounded, just as they had since ancient Greece (luminaries like Bacon believed this process inductively began with careful observation of nature, while others such as Descartes believed that it began with clear and distinct ideas from the mind, which were then deductively considered), they all believed that the underlying premise of their approach was an unwavering commitment to objective observation and analysis. All of their thinking was based on observing the world and their own ideas, without the medieval scholastic baggage of merely providing additional evidence for what had already been "proven." They engaged in objective analysis, experimentation, and intense, real-world scrutiny, valuing curiosity and that deep-seated human desire to discover how the world and society actually worked in practice, not just in theory. This, quite naturally, led to the next logical step of how, and to what extent, scientific discovery and political institutions could improve the world that we all experience.

What is essential to the radical objectivity of the new thinking is the separation of the analysis of problems from the development of policies to solve the problems. Using an objective view of the world, the analysis begins by breaking the observations of the real world and various ideas down into their smallest core elements. Then, and only then, can we begin recognizing and examining patterns throughout these complex issues and identifying the root causes of our challenges. Each element must be evaluated from both a top-down and bottom-up perspective, taking from both sides what is useful and productive, and discarding the rest. Then an accurate understanding of the real world can emerge, allowing us to sharpen and focus our arguments through healthy, open-ended exchanges, circumventing ideological, partisan, and special interest distortion.

Bringing Method to the Madness: Focus on What Works and What Doesn't Work

The second step is to fully develop and implement a new method of political discourse to consistently make better decisions by embracing what works from both the Left and the Right, and eliminating what does not. Once the impractical, distorted, and counterproductive elements are jettisoned, decision makers can consider an entirely new and vast array of workable possibilities, some of which reveal themselves and only become available for consideration after the flawed and failing options have been discarded.

Of course, in political and economic discourse, it is much more difficult to remain steadfastly objective than in the hard sciences, where experiments can more definitively prove or disprove an assertion. At the same time, far too frequently proponents of a particular political or economic position are, in fact, rigidly defending a whole belief structure underpinning their assertion, rather than systematically and objectively working through each issue. Just as there have been throughout history, there are presently a multitude of naturally occurring and perfectly legitimate perspectives. Today, however, the influence of ideological and partisan polarization has converted these pre-analytic opinions into hardened "truths." As President John F. Kennedy presciently declared in 1962, "Too often we . . . enjoy the comfort of opinion without the discomfort of thought." It is clear that most Americans today are more than eager to exchange the comfort of opinion for the discomfort of thought, if the byproduct is durable solutions to our pressing problems, serious structural reform, and sustainable prosperity for future generations.

In order to accomplish this formidable task, however, we must recognize both the unique insights, as well as the potential for error, that each perspective brings to the table. Instead of investing our identities in each ideological and partisan proposition and special interest cause, we must maintain the flexibility to incorporate different ideas based solely on how useful they are to solving the problem at hand. We must further recognize that both sides of the spectrum are vital to our overall understanding of the complex system that is the modern world. As John Stuart Mill described so insightfully in his major work about the unique challenges of freedom and authority, *On Liberty*, the more diversely we challenge our thinking, the better and more well-rounded it becomes. Moreover, Mill asserted that it was only this diversity of objective, open-ended investigation that prevented our ideas from growing ossified, stagnant, and counterproductive. The focus of the Synthesis Revolution is developing a process that consistently incorporates the good from both sides and systematically weeds out the bad.

The final stage of the new method is the process of identifying potential solutions for each of the specific root causes of the various problems under consideration. It is important to evaluate each idea solely on the basis of its usefulness and effectiveness in solving the core problem within the context of society as a whole. Subsequently, each idea should be considered based on a top-down and a bottom-up approach to assess its capacity for effectively addressing each root cause. Any thesis or antithesis must be grounded in clear and objective observations and analysis of the real world. Then, through a free, fair, and productive debate, we can evenhandedly weigh the merits and flaws of each argument, and synthesize only what is useful and meaningful while discarding any elements that are an impediment to durable, workable solutions.

Solutions for Society: Transforming America, One Idea at a Time

The third and final step of the Synthesis Revolution is to combine the new thinking and the new methodology, and to embrace innovation by testing, experimentation, and validating an array of potential solutions, followed by the careful, prudent adoption of the optimal ones. By eschewing ideology, partisan concerns, or special interests, this approach to synthesizing validated, demonstrable, and effective solutions jettisons the comfort of opinion for the discomfort of genuinely objective, critical, and productive thought. Thomas Jefferson famously wrote, "No experiment can be more interesting than that we are now trying, and which we trust will end in establishing the fact, that [people] may be governed by reason and truth. Our first object should therefore be, to leave open ... all avenues to truth." Alexis de Tocqueville shared Jefferson's belief in America as the "Great Experiment" of the modern era.

Political thinkers since Supreme Court Justice Louis Brandeis have also frequently described state and local governments as "laboratories of democracy," where local decision makers explore and test new ideas and determine how effective they are for solving the actual challenges of the real world. The key for the United States to rekindle its innovating spirit in our political dynamic is to once again embrace the shared willingness to intelligently and prudently try new ways of getting things done and blazing new trails. Embracing the process of Synthesis at all levels of government will be nothing short of revolutionary: it will empower decision makers to consider alternatives where the scope and impact would far outstrip the half-measures our politicians and policymakers squabble over today.

The Scope of the Synthesis Revolution

The Synthesis Revolution is first and foremost the coming together of concerned citizens into a coalition whose intent is to address the very real and acute problems facing society today. Americans have become so conditioned to think in polarized terms that to unseat the current, ineffective approach and dissolve the structural barriers within our political dynamic, we must, as Ronald Reagan, our last transformational president, said, provide "a new vision of a better America," an America where the interests of individuals and society as a whole converge into what works and what creates the most value on every level. What unites this coalition is a shared belief in the potency and effectiveness of embracing new thinking and applying a new method for creating the most innovative, productive, and inclusive society on earth. For the first time in decades, this coalition will provide a unified framework with which we can have an honest and meaningful debate about actual, pressing challenges that have festered for decades, combined with an effective mechanism for evaluating various ideas and resolving these challenges. This coalition will transform the political and economic debate from the current quagmire into a productive, results-oriented dialogue, imbued with a new quality of thinking and interaction.

This new vision for a better America begins with drawing a line in the sand and demanding clarity, transparency, and accountability of public servants at all levels of government, and forcing our political leaders to own up to their responsibilities of tackling the serious reforms we need to undertake and have known we need to implement for over a generation. Our coalition will sever the blind adherence to ideology and political parties, and dissolve the influence of special interests. We will build a new political movement of Synthesis based on objective observation and analysis, systematically examining the evidence to identify what is useful and effective in understanding and solving problems and promoting prosperity, and validation of potential solutions through experiment and testing.

The Synthesis Coalition, this body of concerned citizens

focused on solutions, will first emerge through the dynamic interface of new technologies and social media, coalescing into a more organized Society of Synthesis, and eventually gathering steam and taking action through in-person meetings and rallies. As such, this coalition will fundamentally improve our political dynamic by meaningfully shifting the way we think and interact on important political, economic, and societal issues, and by presenting and arguing for practical, demonstrable, and effective solutions. By forcing decision makers to expand their narrow vision and consider real-world solutions for our pressing problems, the Synthesis Revolution will improve our policymaking process while also holding it accountable through effective oversight and removing the ability of our country's leaders to hide behind distorting and counterproductive ideological, partisan, or special interest barriers.

Since the days of ancient Greece and Rome, democracy has always operated on two levels. One is the scope of ideas addressing how we can most effectively organize ourselves and unleash the immense energy of a free people to govern themselves and create prosperity. The other is the scope of power and authority allocated to those in positions of leadership. In order to make permanent change in the effectiveness of our political dynamic, we must address and improve both aspects. Society is already stirring with discontentment and disillusionment over how our political leaders operate and attempt to foster prosperity. The Tea Party and the Occupy Movement have captured just a small portion of the anger and dissatisfaction that exists within the American public. However, protest movements will only succeed insofar as they can become part of the wider dialogue and then improve the outcomes of our political and economic dynamic. Otherwise, they will be limited to short-term effects and will not usher in the type of substantive reform that is so clearly required at this time. The Synthesis Revolution will not only galvanize citizens to act, as other social and political movements have, but it will also reform the current dynamic with new thinking and a new method for addressing real issues and solving difficult problems.

The Impact of the Synthesis Revolution: How New Thinking and New Methods Can Meaningfully Improve Our Lives

In the last thirty years, successive Congresses and presidents have passed tax reforms, entitlement reforms, balanced budget laws, immigration reforms, education reforms, financial reforms, and even health care reforms, but none of these pieces of legislation has led to substantial overall improvement, let alone a transformation, of people's everyday lives. In so many areas of our society, we continue to achieve far less than if our resources were productively utilized. The reason is very simply that once the fanfare, accolades, and photo ops fade away, the influence of ideology, partisan tribalism, and special interests on the fundamental relationship between the tired, failed ideas and those in power continues unabated. The Synthesis Revolution would fundamentally shift this dynamic, enabling our legislative and policymaking efforts to yield significant, even transformative, outcomes.

One of the areas where the Synthesis Revolution would undoubtedly bear fruit is in the financial and economic policy arena, where an honest dialogue and drastic structural reform are profoundly needed. In any market-based economy, the financial sector plays a key role in gathering and allocating capital to its most productive uses. Unfortunately, over the past three decades the financial industry in the United States has gradually gone from being an effective intermediary, competing on the basis of providing the best service and advice to its clients for allocating capital, to focusing exclusively on generating enormous profits for themselves at the expense of their clients and ultimately, as in the 2008 crisis, at the expense of the entire country. Instead of creating value and productively adding to the success of the overall economy, the financial sector has extracted massive amounts of value and misallocated vital resources of our economic system, costing Americans trillions of dollars in net worth and, in the words of former Treasury Secretary Hank Paulson, putting our entire financial system "on the brink" of collapse.

With new thinking and a new method, we can develop and implement durable solutions and create effective and sustainable financial and regulatory policies. Accomplishing this essential goal does not require gargantuan pieces of legislation: the Glass-Steagall Act was fewer than fifty pages long, but along with other straightforward, principles-based regulations, prevented a serious banking crisis for more than fifty years. The real effort is in the innovative thinking and core principles that underpin the actual text of proposed new laws. In other words, effective regulation does not necessitate a heavier regulatory burden; it simply means providing a solid framework of rules and oversight that consistently incentivize adding value through productive intermediation, not merely promoting any activity for which a bank can extract a payment. For a debate about our financial sector to be effective, it must begin with fundamental questions that challenge the prevailing assumptions of how the financial industry is supposed to work, and the predetermined conclusions about what a financial system is supposed to achieve, that have so clearly failed but are continuing to be applied. How do we bring about a productive reconciliation of various ideas, perspectives, and interests within a society focused on generating both progress and stability?

The guiding principle must be to combine the entrepreneurial drive and spirit of innovation of the individual with the legal and regulatory infrastructure that constrains those activities that drain value and add unsustainable risk to our economic system. To accomplish this, we must look at society and the economy as they really are, not as utopian ideological visions that both the Left and the Right have counterproductively and erroneously argued them to be. We need to view our government as the Founding Fathers did, as providing a framework and a foundation in which new ideas and hard work are rewarded, and productivity-draining rent-seeking and the manipulation of political and financial connections are not.

Since the beginning of the modern era, the core prosperity-generating engines of innovation and rising productivity are not byproducts of merely transferring wealth from one segment of society to another, but of creating new ways of doing things that benefit both the individual innovator and society as a whole. The urgent question we must ask ourselves in reflecting on the types of reforms needed in our financial sector is: what are the values and animating purpose that would constitute legitimate foundations for financial institutions to further innovation, productivity, and inclusiveness within society? This is not a question of regulation, but rather a challenge to ourselves and our leaders to clearly define the core values that drive how they really operate and by which stakeholders in society (legislators, policymakers, citizens, shareholders, customers) can hold them accountable for their actions *and the outcomes of that behavior.* Accountability is not just a rare commodity in Washington these days, but on Wall Street as well, as billions of dollars of bonuses were doled out both during and directly after the 2008 crisis.

Considered in this light, it is not a mystery that "too big to fail" banks and the lack of transparency and oversight by financial regulators led to the financial crisis of 2008. In the complex system that is our modern economy, when one segment is not providing its true essential function then the whole system can become dangerously out of balance and in jeopardy of generating enormous bubbles and, as with the last three recessions, a corresponding crisis. The added connectivity of technology and globalization has greatly increased these risks. Until we restore the financial sector to its core function of genuinely competing on the basis of efficiently collecting capital and allocating it to its most productive uses and providing the best service to customers, then it will continue to extract value at the expense of everyone else. Objective observation and analysis often starts with asking tough, and sometimes novel, questions. Considering these issues without ideological distortion helps to shape the debate and expand the realm of possibilities for serious reform of each aspect of our government.

A vital next step would be to explore a variety of possible ways to enable the financial sector to operate based on the new foundational principles we retain after challenging our thinking about the whole industry. Crucially, we need to recognize the insights both perspectives have to offer and keep only what works, discarding what does not. From a top-down perspective, it would be beneficial to discuss basic regulatory and policy principles that could enable the financial sector to operate more productively, and then prudently test these principles before drafting any legislation. From the bottom-up perspective, it would be valuable to observe those aspects that are already working, and what can then be replicated across the whole sector. Moreover, our observations should not be limited to our direct experiences alone: if there is worthy evidence of financial organizations operating effectively and according to the foundational principles needed for a healthy overall economy in another country or in an individual state, it would be most efficient to consider these options as well. Limiting ourselves to homegrown or federal solutions is an artificial constraint that only closes off potential avenues to improvement.

Determining the optimal framework for our financial sector entails synthesizing the most workable top-down ideas with the most effective bottom-up experiments and established practices into the most sound and productive architecture and guiding principles. Some of these principles and part of the architectural blueprint will need to be enshrined in legislation to ensure a stable foundation, though other governance and accountability structures will be part of an ongoing free, fair, and productive debate about best practices, continual adjustment, and ongoing reforms. New developments and innovations within the financial sector will constantly require new responses and revised applications of existing policies.

The Synthesis Revolution not only enhances our ability to learn from history, but also firmly focuses our attention on developing the most innovative, productive, and inclusive economy possible. With new thinking and a new method, we can develop and implement durable solutions, and create effective and sustainable financial and regulatory policies. The key to a useful debate on this issue is to look at the challenge from both perspectives. We must have the bottom-up innovation, drive, and energy that is so necessary in a modern economy, but we must also have the proper rule of law and organizational framework that ensures both free and fair competition so that the financial industry is incentivized to provide the vital function of allocating capital efficiently and productively, not creating bubbles and weighing down healthy companies and various levels of government with unsustainable debt burdens and crippling future liabilities.

Realizing the Promise of Our Founding Fathers and Modernity

To enable us to make these necessary improvements to society, we must replace the draining, polarizing, and distorting focus of ideology, partisan tribalism, and special interests with the new thinking and the new method of the Synthesis Revolution. Synthesis works best when goals and objectives are largely shared, such as our current need to redirect our political and economic debate toward improving our ability to be the most innovative, productive, and inclusive society on earth.

Europe and her offshoots would not have been able to break free of the intellectual and mental shackles of the Middle Ages and develop the framework for all modern scientific, economic, and political advancement, unless they had been able to develop new thinking and a new method for analyzing and solving problems. All of the great thinkers in science, economics, and politics understood that by thinking and interacting in completely new ways they could unleash the unparalleled power of free minds, and the boundless energy of a free people, to greatly enhance the effectiveness of their investigations and increase the well-being of both individuals and society as a whole.

In a similar way, America today will not break free of the

extreme polarization of our political and economic thinking until we embrace the new thinking and the new methodology of the Synthesis Revolution. Just as Americans have done since the days of the Founding Fathers, when a significant inflection point arises, we have the capacity to confront the challenge, overcome it, and flourish once again. Our abilities to invent new and better ways of doing things and repairing our faults are the fundamental keys to our success and, because of that, no other country comes close to America's potential and capacity to lead the world through the twenty-first century and beyond. If we embrace the new way of thinking and the new approach of the Synthesis Revolution, we can unleash the full creative force and productivity of a free, self-governing people in the realization of stability and enormous growth. The only group standing in the way of this New Era of Prosperity is ourselves. And, as we've demonstrated so many times before, we have the capacity, the will, and the commitment to fix our problems and provide a better America for future generations. What is required to fully accomplish this transformation is that we, once again, engage in a Revolution.

Join us in transforming America through improving the way that we make political and economic decisions.

JOIN THE REVOLUTION!

www.SynthesisRevolution.com

ABOUT THE AUTHOR

Thomas "Tom" Rossman has spent his career studying and investigating how people around the world can think and interact more effectively. As a young executive in finance during the 1990's, Rossman was an early champion of up-and-coming markets, investing in the newly emerging Latin American, Chinese and Asian markets far ahead of the crowd. Following Communism's collapse, Rossman took a key role at the leading Turkish Investment Bank, Global Securities, in bringing American capital and investment to the developing markets of the Former Soviet Union, Eastern Europe, Turkey and North Africa. By assisting in the privatization process within Eastern Europe and the Former Soviet Union, Rossman became an important link between Western capital and know-how in the early stages of modernizing these formerly closed economic systems. First as an institutional advisor, and then as an independent consultant, he continued to advocate the sustainable development of democratic and stable free market institutions and expanding economic opportunity throughout the region. More recently, Rossman has provided a similar advisory role to family holding companies and financial companies in the Middle East seeking to most effectively navigate through the volatility of the current financial crisis.

Mr. Rossman has spoken on these topics at conferences around the world in such diverse places as London, New York, Istanbul, Baku, Almaty, Bishkek, Tashkent, Stockholm, Washington DC and Houston and he has lived in both Turkey and Kuwait. He studied religion and history at Nyack College in Nyack, New York and did his masters work in international relations at the Fletcher School of Law and Diplomacy in Boston, Massachusetts.

www.ingramcontent.com/pod-product-compliance
Lightning Source LLC
Chambersburg PA
CBHW022131280326
41933CB00007B/642